Devon Place Names

Robert Hesketh

Bossiney Books • Launceston

First published 2008 by
Bossiney Books Ltd, Langore, Launceston, Cornwall, PL15 8LD
www.bossineybooks.com

ISBN 978-1-899383-98-6

Printed in Great Britain by St Austell Printing Company Ltd

Introduction

English place names reflect the history of England; they are as much a part of our heritage as the English language and the English countryside – and inseparable from both.

In Devon, the English flair for naming places is seen to the full in a rich tapestry woven from the Old English, Old Norse, Latin, Norman French and British (parent of modern Cornish and Welsh) languages. Devon place names are part of a landscape of special character, with its *combes* and *tors*, its *cotts*, *cleaves* and *hoes*.

Every Devon place name has a story to tell, mostly a very old story going back well over 1000 years to the Saxon settlement. These reflect successive layers of conquest and settlement, telling us a great deal about our ancestors, the languages they spoke, their names and the lives they led. Often, they tell us why people settled where they did, for instance near a water supply in Og*well*, for defence at Sid*bury* ('fort by the river Sid'), at fording points such as Bide*ford*, or bridging places like Kings*bridge*.

Only a few Devon names such as Kingsbridge, Sandford, Heathfield and the river Otter are plain in modern English. This book focuses on the hidden meanings which often lurk behind much changed forms. Some need a full translation, as even Old English – the raw material for most Devon names – is largely a foreign language. Snapper, for instance, derives from the Old English *snaep*, meaning 'boggy land'.

Fortunately, many names contain widespread elements such as *leah* meaning a woodland clearing; *combe* 'a valley'; *torr* 'rocky hill'; and *cleave* 'cliff'. These elements are listed in the glossary. Often, they are strikingly apt. Even after the changes wrought by time, Lustleigh ('Leofgiest's *leah* or clearing') is surrounded by thick woodland in a valley south of Higher Combe and Middle Combe. The cliffs of nearby Lustleigh Cleave impress us as much as they did our ancestors.

The pronunciation and spelling of most names have changed over the centuries, often radically. Only by carefully studying and comparing early written records of places can scholars really explain their names. *Domesday Book*, the great survey of his newly conquered kingdom ordered by William I in 1086, has been exceptionally useful, a bench-mark in place name studies. Various charters, deeds

and other medieval documents have helped too. The Anglo Saxon Chronicle, first written in the 9th century, gives the earliest spelling of many names. The Venerable Bede's *History of the Church* gives some others, whilst Roman writers, including Tacitus, Caesar and Ptolemy, recorded a few names (including Exeter) for the first time.

However, some place names are uncertain or disputed. Sometimes, there are few or no early spellings to help. A few names defy explanation entirely. They seem not to relate to any known language. Devon's river Bovey is an example.

Although Rome conquered most of Britain, including Devon, the Roman administrators did little to change existing British place names and most Latin names in Devon, such as Buckland Monachorum, came from medieval scribes. There were few Roman settlers to name places anyway – probably the British climate was a deterrent. Matters were very different with the larger numbers of Germanic settlers who followed.

Devon names for villages and farms are predominantly Old English, suggesting that Saxon settlement, or at least cultural and linguistic influence, was dominant. Possibly the Britons adopted the English language and continued to live side by side with the Saxons, probably as serfs in some places. A more radical view is that most Britons were driven out of Devon.

Devon was the last and most western county to be settled by the Saxons. It was not until 712 that they established a boundary west of the Tamar. Beyond, in most but not all of Cornwall, British settlement names predominate. In Devon the use of British is largely confined to natural features – more than a quarter of Devon's rivers, including the major ones, have British names.

By contrast, the Vikings made little impression on Devon's place names, which gives them a very different flavour from those of East Anglia, Northern England and the East Midlands. There, Danish and Norwegian names are legion, especially those ending with *by*, *thorp*, *thwaite* and *toft*, because Scandinavians settled in large numbers. Devon, where the Vikings only raided, has few Norse names, mainly confined to the coast – Lundy and Oldstone, for instance.

The Norman conquest of 1066 began the last major phase of place naming. Most Norman French names in Devon are from powerful feudal families, joined to earlier Saxon or British place names, such

as Nymet *Tracey*, Sampford *Courtenay*, Berry *Pomeroy* and Churston *Ferrers*.

Usually, the Normans simply took over existing names, though some places, such as the Normans' new *Rougemont* ('Red Hill') Castle in Exeter, needed new ones. Devon has the largest concentration of post-Conquest (1066) names in England. Some are medieval clarifications. Thus two farmstead settlements (*tuns*) on the river Teign became today's Kingsteignton and Bishopsteignton. Similarly, Littlehempston was distinguished from nearby Broadhempston.

A few Devon names are (by place name standards) very modern. Devonport was renamed by royal permission in 1824. Before then it was known as 'Dock'. Princetown was so called after the dissolute Prince of Wales, later George IV. More inventively, the new Victorian coastal resort Westward Ho! commemorates Charles Kingsley's swashbuckling Devon novel.

A great deal of Devon's history can be read in its place names. Many show the crucial importance of farming. Cowick 'cow farm', Chawleigh 'calves' clearing', Sheepwash (it means what it says!) and Swincombe 'swine valley', show that stock rearing was widespread. Plympton 'plum tree farm' and Appledore 'apple tree' remind us of fruit farming, Watcombe 'wheat valley' and the many Bartons – 'barley farms' or 'grain stores' – speak of common crops. Industry is recalled in names such as Budleigh Salterton 'salt farm', and trade in many street titles like Goldsmith Street and Milk Street, Exeter.

A line of *burys* ('hillforts') near the Dorset border, including Musbury, Sidbury and Membury, reveal old tensions between the *Dumnonii* and the neighbouring *Durotriges* – Devon and Dorset respectively are named after these British tribes. Bretonside in Plymouth commemorates the defeat of a Breton raid in 1403, whilst Countess Wear (Exeter) is named after Isabella de Fortibus, Countess of Devon, who constructed a weir across the Exe here in 1286.

Among the more than 500 place names in this book are many Saxon personal names. Most, like Lympstone ('Leofwine's farm'), recall otherwise forgotten people who must once have been powerful locally. Such names are often preserved, as are many Old English words, only in place names. Nearly all are male, but a few such as Beaworthy 'Beaga's enclosure' honour women; probably this is an accurate reflection of women's subordinate role in Saxon society.

5

As well as towns and villages, hills and rivers, I have included a selection of street names from Exeter and Plymouth and a good sprinkling of minor names chosen for intrinsic interest and sometimes bizarre flavour. Read on for Black Dog, Lillicrap, Guzzle Down, Camel's Head, Warfleet, Castle Drogo, Coppa Dolla and Grimspound...

I hope you enjoy studying Devon's place names and are able to visit some intriguing places. Ordnance Survey maps are immensely useful in finding them and seeing how they describe the local environment. If the subject really grabs you, there are several very well written books (see bibliography), and the English Place Name Society is to be recommended.

Glossary

Abbreviations used in the dictionary are explained below, along with some words ('elements') commonly found in English place names. Nearly all are Old English (OE), but most need to be translated because Old English was very different from modern English. Over the centuries, some elements came to mean several things. Scholars look at early spellings, local topography and history to gain a better understanding of particular place names.

Bearu   OE 'wood or grove'. Over 100 examples in Devon, where it is especially common. Sometimes rendered 'Beer', 'Beare' or 'Bere'. 20 per cent of names with *bearu* include the name of an early owner.

Beorg   OE 'hill'.

Boc-land   OE 'land granted by charter'.

Brad   OE 'broad or big'.

Burh   OE 'fortified place'. Found as 'berry' or 'bury', this usually refers to prehistoric hill forts in Devon, but can also refer to Roman, Saxon or medieval fortifications.

Cot   OE 'cottage, hut, shelter'.

Cumb   'valley', usually rendered 'combe', is the second most common Devon place name element after *tun*. It may have been borrowed from British into OE, or it may have been a native OE word.

DB   'Domesday Book', 1086. William the Conqueror's massive survey of his new kingdom provides a wealth of information and many early spellings. It is a benchmark for place name historians.

Ford   OE 'ford'.

Haeg   OE 'enclosure', related to the modern French *haye*, 'hedge'.

Ham   OE 'homestead, village, manor, estate'. Modern English 'home' is derived from it. Do not confuse it with Hamm.

Hamm   OE 'land hemmed in by marsh or water'.

Hoh   OE 'place at the spur of land'. Rendered 'hoe'.

Ing   OE means 'place belonging to' or 'people of' if it is a suffix (comes at the end of a word).

Ing   OE means 'associated with' or 'called after' if it is a connective particle (comes in the middle of a word).

7

-ingtun   OE 'farm or settlement associated with [such a person]'. See also *tun* below.

Leah   OE 'woodland clearing or glade'. Later 'open pasture or meadow', rendered 'leigh', 'lee', 'ly' and 'lea'.

Naess   OE and ON *Nes*, 'a promontory or headland'.

OE   'Old English', with its various dialects (West Saxon in Devon), is commonly known as 'Anglo-Saxon'. The language changed radically after the Norman Conquest of 1066, partly under the influence of Norman French. Some OE words are recognisable to modern readers, many are not.

ON   'Old Norse': the languages (and cultures) of the Danish and Norwegians were closely related to Old English.

Penn   Can mean either 'fold or animal enclosure' if it is from Old English, or 'head, end, hill or chief' if it comes from British. Compare Ipplepen and Pinhoe.

PND   *The Place Names of Devon* (see Bibliography).

Saelt   OE 'salt', see Salcombe.

Saltere   OE 'saltworker' or 'salt workers', see Budleigh Salterton.

Sealh   OE 'willow tree, or sallow'.

Stan   OE 'stone'.

Stoc   OE 'outlying settlement or farmstead, secondary settlement'.

Stocc   OE 'tree trunk, stump'.

Stow   OE 'place, assembly place and (especially) holy place'.

Torr   OE 'rock or rocky hill'.

Tun   The most common OE place name element, but its meaning for a particular place varies from 'farmstead or village' to 'estate or manor' when joined to a personal name. Usually rendered 'ton'.

Wic   OE 'dwelling', 'hamlet' or 'village' in its general sense, but usually 'specialised farm or dairy farm' and rendered 'Week' or 'Weeke'.

Wiella   (also *wella*) OE 'spring or stream'. Rendered 'well'.

Worthig   (also *worth*) OE 'enclosure or enclosed settlement'. Rendered 'worthy' or 'worth'.

Wudu   OE 'wood'.

The Dictionary

A

Abbotsham: 'Abbot's hemmed in land', OE.

Abbotskerswell: 'The Abbot's spring or stream where watercress grows', OE (see Kingskerswell).

Alphington: 'Aelf's or Aelfwulf's farm/settlement', OE.

Anstey (East and West): Probably 'steep, narrow footpath', OE.

Appledore: 'Apple tree', OE.

Arlington: 'Estate associated with the man Aelffrith', OE.

Ashburton: 'Village or farm by the brook where ash trees grow', OE. The river Ashburn is now called the Yeo (see below).

Ashprington: 'Farm or settlement connected with a man called Aescbeorht or Aescbeorn', OE.

Aveton Gifford: 'Farmstead on the River Avon'. The Giffard family were here in the 13th century. (See Compton Gifford and Weare Gifford.)

Avon (river): 'River', British. This common name may result from people calling their local river simply 'the river' – as do modern Londoners, for example.

Axe (river): 'Water', British. Like many river names, Axe is very plain. (Similar to Exe and Yeo – see below.)

Axminster: 'Monastery or large church on river Axe', OE. (See Exminster.)

Axmouth: 'At the mouth of river Axe' (above), OE.

Aylesbeare: 'Grove belonging to a man called Aegel', OE.

B

Babbacombe: 'The combe or valley belonging to Babba', OE. There are two places with this name in Devon.

Bampton: Probably '*tun* (farm/settlement) of the dwellers by the bath or hot spring', OE.

Barnfield (Exeter): Named after the field between Southernhay (below) and Larkbeare Brook (below).

Barnstaple: Debated. Predates 'staple' meaning 'trading-place' by 500 years. Possibly 'Battle axe post' (signifying a meeting place) or 'Bearded post, used as a land or seamark'. Both OE.

Bartholomew Street (Exeter): Formerly 'Britayne', part of the district (the 'West Quarter') occupied by the conquered British in Saxon times. The churchyard was called Bartholomew Yard on St Bartholomew's Day 1637 and thus the street got its name.

Barton: 'Barley farm' or 'outlying grange where corn is stored', OE. There are six places with this name in Devon. In the 13th century, barton developed the additional meaning of 'demesne farm'.

Beaford: 'Gadfly ford', OE. (See Pyworthy for another insect name.)

Beaworthy: 'Enclosure belonging to a woman called Beaga', OE.

Beer: 'Grove'. Beer comes from the OE word *bearu* and has nothing to do with drink! Many Devon place names contain this word, spelled variously 'beer', 'bere' and 'beare'.

Beesands: Probably from Beeson, a nearby village, which possibly means 'Beade's farm', OE.

Bellever: 'Ford over the stream' (see *wiella*) as shown by spelling 'Welford' in 1355, OE.

Belstone: 'Bell shaped stone', OE.

Bere Ferrers: 'Grove belonging to the Ferrers family.' OE *bearu* + Norman family name. (See Churston Ferrers and Newton Ferrers.)

Berry: 'Fortification', OE *burh*. 14 places in Devon are called 'Berry', eg Berry Head, plus combinations (see below). 'Berry' was applied to fortifications from the pre-historic through the Roman and Anglo-Saxon periods to medieval fortified houses, towns and boroughs.

Berrynarbor: 'At the fortification', OE + family name Nerebert (the 13th century owners).

Berry Pomeroy: Similar to Berrynarbor, 'At the fortification' OE + Norman manorial name de Pomerei. (See Stockleigh Pomeroy.)

Bickington: 'Farm or settlement connected with a man called Beocca or Bucca', OE. Bickington Abbots was possessed by Hartland Abbey. High Bickington is on high ground.

Bickleigh: Either 'pointed ridge woodland clearing' or 'Bica's woodland clearing', OE. (There are two in Devon.)

Bideford: OE. Various explanations have been offered, including 'By the ford' and 'Bidda's ford'. Possibly it signifies 'Ford at the stream called Byd', or refers to the shape of the valley it lies in.

Bigbury: 'Bica's fort', OE personal name + 'bury', comparable with 'berry' (above).

Bishop's Tawton: 'Farm or settlement on the river Taw', owned by the Bishop (of Exeter), OE. (See Taw.)

Bishopsteignton: 'Farmstead on the river Teign (see below) owned by the Bishop (of Exeter)'.

Blackdown Hills: 'Black Down/hill', OE. Comparable with Blagdon.

Black Dog: Two Devon hamlets are named after pubs called the Black Dog. No relation to Snapper (below).

Blackawton: Either 'Farm belonging to Afa' or 'Farm/settlement on the river Avon'. (Avon may be an old name for the river Gara.) Recorded as *Auetona* in DB. *Blake* (black) added 1281, perhaps because of local soil or vegetation, maybe to distinguish it from Aveton Gifford (see above).

Blackpool: Self-explanatory. There are two such places in Devon.

Blagdon: See Blackdown.

Bolt Head: Probably the land called Bolt stretched to Bolt Tail. *Bolt* is OE for 'arrow', as in the phrase 'bolt from the blue'. The straight stretch of high coast over Bolberry might suggest an arrow, with its head and tail. Bolberry was recorded as *Boltesberia* 1086 and *Boltebyry* in 1224, the 'berry' referring to a vanished fortification.

Bonhay (Exeter): 'Good enclosure'; French *bon* and OE *haeg*. The earliest spelling is 1558, so its original meaning may have been different. (See Northernhay and Shilhay.)

Bovey (river): A pre-English, possibly even a pre-British term. Like many very ancient words, it may never be explained.

Bovey Tracey: Recorded *Sutbovi* ('South Bovey') in 1219, it was held by the de Tracey family (from Tracey Bocage or Tracey-sur-Mer, Normandy) in the 13th century. North Bovey is up river. (See Nymet Tracey and Newton Tracy, named from the same family.)

Bowhill (Exeter): 'Curved hill', recorded 1249.

Bradninch: Either 'At the broad ash' or 'At the broad oak', OE.

Bradworthy: 'Broad enclosure', OE *brad* + worthig.

Branscombe: 'Branoc's Valley', British personal name + combe. (See Braunton and Combe.)

Bratton Clovelly: 'Farm or settlement of newly broken land', OE. Held by the Clavill family, but the spelling was influenced by Clovelly (below).

Bratton Fleming: As above. Held by Baldwin le Fleming ('of Flanders') in 1242. The same family held Stoke Fleming (below).

Braunton: Either 'Farm where broom grows' or 'Branoc's farm'. (See Branscombe.)

Bray: 'Hill', British. The river name derives from the settlement.

Brendon: 'Broom Hill', OE *brom* + *dun*.

Brentor: 'Rocky hill, high place'. This apparently hybrid name combines OE *torr*, possibly with the British *brente*. (See South Brent.)

Bretonside (Plymouth): The part of Plymouth outside St Martyn's Gate occupied by a Breton raiding force in 1403 has been Bretonside ever since – though a modern council has moved the name uphill into old Plymouth (bus station area) and muddled matters.

Bridestowe: 'Holy place of St Bride or Brigid'. Irish saint's name + OE *stow*. (See Virginstow.)

Bridford: Uncertain. Could be from St Bride, as at Bridestow, but OE *bryd* can mean either bird or bride. Surprisingly, expert opinion opts for 'ford suitable for brides' – a ford easy to cross.

Brixham: 'Brioc's farmstead or enclosure', British personal name + ham.

Brixton: Probably 'Brioc's farm (*tun*).'

Broadclyst: 'Farm on river Clyst'. 'Broad', meaning great, was first recorded in 1372, distinguishing it from other Clyst villages. (See Broadhempston, Bradworthy and Clyst.)

Broadhembury: 'Great, high fort', OE. Nearby Hembury Fort, is Devon's largest earthwork. (See Payhembury.)

Broadhempston: 'Farm belonging to a man called Haeme', OE. *Brad* 'broad' distinguishes it from the nearby village, Littlehempston (see below).

Broadwoodwidger: 'Big wood belonging to the Wyger family' (who held the manor in the 13th century).

Brownsham (Hartland): 'Brun's settlement or hemmed in land', OE.

Buckfast: 'Sheltered place, a fastness, for bucks' (male deer), OE.

Buckfastleigh: The same as Buckfast + OE *leah*, a woodland clearing.

Buckland (East and West): OE *boc-land*, meaning 'book land' granted by Anglo Saxon royal charter with certain rights and privileges.

Buckland-in-the-Moor: *Bochelanda* in DB and *Boklonde Inthemore* in 1334 is on Dartmoor.

Buckland Brewer: Was owned by the Briwerre family, 13th century.

Buckland Filleigh: Held by the de Fyleleye family, 13th century.

Buckland Monachorum: Latin 'of the monks', referring to nearby Buckland Abbey, founded 1278. (See Zeal Monachorum.)

Buckland Tout Saints: Was connected with the Tuz Seinz family, 1238.

Bucks Cross and **Mills:** 'Land granted by charter' (similar to the various Bucklands above).

Budleigh Salterton: 'Budda's clearing', OE personal name + *leah*. Salterton was 'Salt workers farm', OE words *saltere* + *tun*. Salt was extracted from sea water by evaporation. (See East Budleigh, Salcombe Regis and Woodbury Salterton.)

Burgh Island: Derived from OE *beorg*, 'a hill'.

Butterleigh: 'Butter Meadow', OE. (*Leah* is used not in its usual sense of 'woodland clearing', but in its later sense of 'meadow'.)

C

Cadbury: 'Cada's fortification' ie Cadbury Castle near Thorverton. This OE personal name is associated with other Iron Age hillforts in neighbouring Somerset. Cada may have been a mythical figure.

Calverleigh: 'Bare wood clearing', OE.

Camel's Head (Plymouth): Uncertain. Probably British, possibly connected with Camulos, the name of a British deity. Recorded as 'Kemel' in 1286. The theory it was named after the 19th century pub called the Camel's Head (demolished 1988) seems improbable – the reverse is more likely.

Castle Drogo: The 20th century castle near Drewsteignton was built by Julius Drewe, who gave it the Latin form of his name 'Drogo'. It is thought that a Norman, Drogo, was granted land near Teignton (ie Drewsteignton) and the anglicised form of his name was added to the village, recorded *Teyngton Drue*, 1275.

Cattedown and **Cattewater (Plymouth):** Derived from the animal name and recorded as la Catte in 1249. Possibly some physical feature of the district suggested the animal or wild cats lived there.

Chagford: OE, 'Ford where broom or gorse grows'.

Challacombe: 'Cold valley', OE.

Chambercombe (Ilfracombe): 'Valley (OE *cumb*)' associated with de Chambernon family, recorded here in 1321.

Chawleigh: 'Calves' clearing', OE *cealf* + *leah*.

Cheriton Bishop: 'Church farm/settlement' owned by Bishops of Exeter, OE. (See Churston Ferrers.)

Cheriton Fitzpaine: Held by the Fitz Payn family in 13th century.

Chipshop: Possibly OE 'Log-built shed or workshop'. First noted 1765 – very late. The 1841 Census shows all the men and boys of Chipshop employed as blacksmiths and carpenters ('chippies'). An alternative explanation is offered for the Chipshop Inn – that local miners were paid in tokens or 'chips' commonly redeemable at company shops.

Chittlehamholt: OE, 'Wood of the dwellers in the valley'.

Chittlehampton: OE, 'Valley dwellers' farm settlement'.

Christow: 'Christian holy place', OE *christen* + *stow*. (See Jacobstowe, Churchstow and Instow.)

Chudleigh: Either 'Ciedda's (personal name) clearing' or 'Clearing in a hollow', OE.

Chudleigh Knighton: 'Farmstead or village of the young thanes (noblemen) or retainers', OE *cniht* + *tun*. (See Knightshayes.)

Chulmleigh: 'Ceolmund's clearing', OE personal name + *leah.*

Churchstow: 'Holy place with a church', OE. (See Jacobstowe, Christow and Instow.)

Churston Ferrers: 'Church farm' (OE) held by Hugh de Ferreris in 1303. (See Newton Ferrers and Cheriton Bishop.)

Clampitt: 'Muddy pit or hollow', OE *clam*, Devon dialect *cloam*

Clifton (Dartmouth): 'Farm or settlement by the cliff', OE.

Clovelly: Uncertain, probably 'ravine near the hill resembling a wheel rim', OE. (See Bratton Clovelly.)

Clyst (river): British, similar to rivers Clyde (Scotland) and Clydach (Wales), probably 'clean stream'. Clyst St George, Clyst St Lawrence, Clyst St Mary (all church dedications) and Clyst Hydon (held by de Hidune family in the 13th century) are on its banks. (See also Broadclyst.)

Cockington: Probably 'Estate associated with Cocca', OE personal name + *ingtun.*

Coffinswell: 'Spring or stream'. The Coffin family held the manor in 12th century. OE + Norman surname.

Coleton Fishacre: 'Colla's Farm'. Egidius de Fyssacre held the manor in 1303.

Coly (river): British, possibly 'narrow'.

Colyford: 'Ford over the Coly'.

Colyton: 'Farmstead on the Coly'. British river name + *tun.*

Combe: OE *cumb* means 'valley'. Widespread place and surname, especially in the West Country, which has many valleys and rocky hills (see Tor below).

Combe Martin: 'Valley', held by Robert, son of Martin, in 1133.

Combe Raleigh: 'Valley' held by de Ralegh family in 13th century.

Combeinteignhead: 'Valley estate of ten hides', recorded as *Comba* in DB and *Cumbe in Tenhide* in 1227. 'Combe' = valley, 'hide' = land supporting one household, usually about 120 acres. Despite the spelling, there is no connection in the place name to the nearby river Teign. (See Stokeinteignhead; also Bishopsteignton, Kingsteignton and Teignmouth).

Compton Gifford (Plymouth): 'Valley farm or settlement', OE *tun* + combe. Held by the Giffard family. (See Aveton Gifford and Weare Gifford.)

Coppa Dolla: Corruption of 'Coppiced alder'. Farm and inn near Broadhempston.

Cornwood: 'Cranes' or herons' wood', OE.

Cornworthy: Either 'Enclosure where corn was grown' or 'enclosure frequented by cranes', from OE *worthig*, an enclosure.

Cotleigh: 'Cotta's woodland clearing'. OE personal name + *leah*.

Countess Wear (Exeter): Named after Isabella de Fortibus, Countess of Devon, who constructed a weir across the Exe here, 1286.

Countisbury: Probably 'Fortified place at a hill called Cunet' or 'Cynuit's hill'. OE *burh* + uncertain British place or personal name.

Cowick (Exeter): 'Cow farm', OE.

Coxside (Plymouth): Probably 'Cokke's quarter'. Richard Cokke was recorded here in 1468.

Crediton: 'Farm on the river Creedy'.

Creedy (river): 'Winding', British.

Crownhill (Plymouth): A self-explanatory modern name, but possibly a polite Victorian substitution for the insulting old name Nackershole, recorded 1765. (See Knacker's Knowle.)

Croyde: 'Headland', OE *cryde*.

Cruwys Morchard: 'Great wood', British *mor* + *ced*. Held by de Crues family in 13th century. (See Morchard Bishop.)

Cullompton: 'Farm (*tun*) on the river Culm'.

Culm (river): Probably British, corresponding to Welsh *cwlm* and Cornish *colm*, meaning 'knot, tie', referring to the river's twists and loops.

Culmstock: 'Outlying farm on the river Culm', OE *stoc*.

Culm Davy: 'Davy's valley'. Recorded 'Combe Davy' 1285. David de Wydeworth held the manor in 1242. The modern spelling is derived from the river Culm, showing how deceptive place names can be.

D

Dalwood: 'Valley wood'. OE *dael* corresponding to ON *dalr* (found mainly in northern England, eg Yorkshire Dales) + OE *wudu*.

Darracott (Georgeham): Probably OE 'Doda's cottage'. Doda held the nearby manor of Saunton (below). The Darracotts in Welcombe and Great Torrington have the same derivation.

Dart (river): British, 'river where oaks grow'.

Dartington: 'Farm on river Dart', British river name + OE *tun*.

Dartmoor: 'Moor of the Dart', OE *mor*.

Dartmouth: 'Mouth of the Dart', OE *mutha*.

Dawlish: From British river name, 'dark stream'.

Dawlish Warren: OE *warenne* 'Game Park'. Recorded as *Warenna in Manerio de Douelis* in 1280.

Dean Prior: 'Valley', OE *denu*. Held by Plympton Priory.

Denbury: 'Fortification of the *Defnas*', the Devonians. (See Devon.)

Devon: 'Territory of the Devonians', OE tribal name *Defnas* from British *Dumnonii*. The Dumnonians' original territory included what became Devon, Cornwall and probably part of western Somerset.

Devonport: Was known as Plymouth Dock until 1824.

Diptford: 'Deep ford', OE.

Dittisham: 'Dyddi's village' or 'Dyddi's hemmed-in land', OE personal name + *ham* or *hamm*.

Doddiscombsleigh: Originally 'The woodland clearing', OE *leah*. The Doddescumb family name was added because they held the manor.

Dog Village: Modern name, ie 'Village known for dogs' (see Black Dog).

Drake's Island (Plymouth): Honours Sir Francis Drake (1540-96). Formerly, it was St Nicholas' Island, with a chapel of that name.

Drewsteignton: 'Drew's farm on the river Teign'. (See Teign and Castle Drogo.)

Dunchideock: 'Wooded fortification', British.

Dunkeswell: Either 'Duduc's or Dunnuc's spring/stream' or 'Hedge sparrow spring/stream', OE. (Dunnock is still used for 'hedge sparrow.')

Dunsford: 'Dun's Ford', OE personal name + ford.

Duryard (Exeter): 'Deer fold'. It was a hunting park of the Anglo-Saxon kings.

E

East Budleigh: Probably 'Budda's clearing', OE personal name Budda + *leah*. (See Budleigh Salterton and Woodbury Salterton.)

East(a)cott: 'East cottages', OE *cot*. There are 10 in Devon. (See Westacott, Northcott, Southcott, Uppacott.)

Easton: 'East farm or settlement', OE *tun*. There are 5 in Devon. (See Weston, Norton, Sutton, Upton.)

Ebford (Woodbury): Was originally Ebworthy, 'Ebba's enclosure'. The modern form, first seen 1630, probably derives from the Clyst being fordable at ebb tide. (See Efford.)

Efford (Plymouth): Probably 'Ford passable at ebb tide', referring to a passage over the Plym.

Egg Beer (Cheriton Bishop): 'Ecga's Wood' OE personal name + *bearu*. It has nothing to do with eggs or beer.

Egg Buckland: 'Heca's Charter land' held by a man called Heca in DB. (See Buckland.)

Ellacombe (Torquay): 'Ella's valley' or 'Elder tree valley', OE.

Endicott: 'Far cottage or beyond the cottage', OE *cot*. (See Northcott.)

Ermington: 'Farm on the river Erme' or 'Earma's farm', OE. Possibly, Ermington gave its name to the river Erme.

Ernesettle (Plymouth): Probably 'Eagle's Seat', OE, or 'Seat of a man called Earn'.

Exbourne: Either 'Cuckoo stream' or 'Gaec's (OE personal name) stream'. Exbourne lies near the Hole Brook, not the river Exe (below).

Exe (river): 'Water', British river name from Isca. Mutated to Esca. (See Axe and Exeter.)

Exeter: 'Fortified Roman settlement on the Exe' (British river name). Recorded in Greek as Isca around AD150, the settlement was at first known by its British river name. The OE *ceaster* (fort) was added later. The Exanceaster of 894 and Excestre of 1086 were smoothed to Exeter by 1547.

Exminster: 'River Exe monastery or large church' OE *mynster*. (See Axminster.)

Exmoor: 'Moor (OE *mor*) of river Exe'.

Exmouth: 'Mouth (OE *mutha*) of river Exe'.

Exwick (Exeter): 'Specialised farm on the Exe', OE (see Exe).

F

Feniton: 'Farm or settlement by Vine Water'. British river name 'boundary water' (it forms part of the boundary of Ottery parish) + *tun*.

Fenny Bridges: 'Bridge over Vine Water' (above).

Fernworthy: 'Bracken enclosure (OE *worthy*)'.

Fingle: OE stream name, possibly 'hold or catch'.

Ford: For obvious reasons this is a very common OE name. (There are 51 in Devon alone.) Its meaning is unchanged.

Ford (Plymouth): Was probably the home of Nicholas de la Forde in 1238. The ford was over a creek of the Hamoaze (below).

Fremington: 'Farm or settlement connected with Fremi or Fremma', OE.

Friar's Lane (Plymouth): The Friars Minor had a house here.

Frithelstock: 'Frithulack's outlying settlement', OE personal name + *stoc*.

G

Galmpton: 'Farm of rent-paying peasants', OE. (There are two places of this name in Devon.)

Gandy Street (Exeter): Originally Currestreet, possibly 'Street where leather is curried (cured)' or 'Dog Street'. Named Gandy Lane in 18th century after local property owners.

Gappah: 'Goat path', OE.

Georgeham: 'Hemmed in land', OE *hamm* + church dedication.

Germansweek: 'Specialised farm' (see Week) + later church dedication to St Germanus (Latin).

Gidleigh: 'Gydda's clearing', OE personal name + *leah*.

Gittisham: Either 'Gyddi's homestead/village' or 'Gyddi's hemmed in land', OE personal name + *ham* or *hamm*.

Goldsmith Street (Exeter): Medieval artisans usually grouped together and streets were often named after them. (See Waterbeer Street, Milk Street, Smith Street and Wolsdon Street.)

Goodleigh: 'Goda's woodland clearing', OE personal name + *leah*. (There are two places of this name in Devon.)

Goodrington: 'Godhere's estate', OE personal name + *ing* + *tun*.

Greenaway (in Gidleigh parish): Owned by Sir Ralph de Grenewaysfote ('Green Ways Foot') in 1244.

Greenway (in Churston Ferrers parish): Recorded *la Greneway*, 1328, 'Green Road'.

Grimspound: Possibly 'Grimr's pound'. Old Norse names are rare in Devon, but this is from *Grimr*, an alternative name for the Norse God, Odin.

Guzzle Down (Brixham parish): 'Goose spring', recorded *Gosewille* 1333.

H

Haldon (hills): Uncertain, possibly from OE words for 'look out hill' or 'holy place'. PND suggests OE *'hail'*, but this makes little sense.

Halwell and Halwill: 'Holy Well', OE.

Hamoaze (Plymouth): 'Ham ooze or mud', OE. The Hamoaze originally referred to the muddy creek that ran up to Ham Manor in Weston, but now includes the Tamar from Saltash to Plymouth Sound.

Harbourne (river): 'Pleasant stream', OE.

Harberton: 'Farm or settlement on the river Harbourne', OE.

Harcombe: 'Hare valley' in Chudleigh and Sidbury parishes, but Harcombe Bottom near Uplyme (*Hertecomb*, 1538) means 'Hart Valley'. OE.

Hardness (Dartmouth): 'Mooring (hard) by the promontory', OE.

Harford: Same derivation as Harpford below.

Harpford: 'Ford on the army road', OE *here-paeth* (comparable with Hereford in the Midlands).

Hartland: Probably 'Farm or settlement on the stags' peninsula', OE.

Hatherleigh: 'Hawthorn or heathery wood clearing', OE.

Heanton Punchardon: 'At the high farm or settlement', OE *heah* + *tun*. Robert de Ponte Cardonis held it in 1086.

Heavitree: Uncertain. Possibly 'Hefa's tree' or 'head tree'.

Heddon: 'Hill where heather grows', OE (4 places in Devon).

Heddon's Mouth Cleave: As above + OE *cleave* 'cliff or steep slope'.

Hele: 'Nook, recess, remote valley', OE. There are 18 Heles in Devon. Ascertaining the exact meaning of each one is difficult.

Hemyock: Possibly an old stream name or 'Hemma's river bend', OE.

Hennock: 'At the high oak', OE.

Hexworthy: 'Hext's enclosure'. Personal name (William Hexta was recorded here in 1417) + *worthy*. Hext remains a Devon surname.

Highampton: 'High farmstead', OE.

Highweek: 'Specialised farm or trading centre/village on high ground', OE. Recorded *Teyngewike* in 1200, referring to the nearby river Teign. (See Week.)

Hockworthy: 'Hocca's enclosure', OE personal name + *worth*.

Hoe: OE *hoh* 'rocky spur of land', a common Devonian coastal feature as in Plymouth Hoe. (See Martinhoe, Mortehoe and Trentishoe – all on rocky spurs.)

Holcombe (near Dawlish): 'Hollow or deep valley', OE.

Holcombe Burnell: Held by Ralph, son of Bernard in 1242. 'Bernard' was corrupted to Burnell.

Holcombe Rogus: Held by one Rogo in DB.

Hole: Usually 'hollow' and a common OE place and surname, eg Thomas Attahole lived at Hole Pit Coppice, Branscombe in 1307.

Holne: 'Holly tree', OE *holegn*.

Holsworthy: 'Heald's enclosure', OE personal name + *worthig.*

Honeychurch: 'Huna's church'. Devon place names with 'Honey' include Honeycliff, Honeyford, Honeyland and Honeywell (giving surname Honeywill). They derive either from OE *hunig* (honey) or personal name Huna. (See Honiton.)

Honicknowle (Plymouth): Probably 'Hana's or Haneca's Hill', OE personal name + *cnoll. Hana* may mean 'wild bird, cock'.

Honiton: 'Huna's farm', OE personal name and *tun.* (See Honeychurch.)

Hope (Inner and Outer): OE *Hop*, 'Remote enclosed land, valley amidst fens or marshes, wasteland'. *Hop* may also explain Hope's Nose, Torquay.

Hound Tor: *Hundatora* in DB and *Hundetorre* in 1238, OE. Thus, the tor's fancied resemblance to, or association with, a pack of hounds is ancient.

I

Iddesleigh: 'Eadwig's or Eadwulf's woodland clearing', OE.

Ilfracombe: 'Aelfred's valley (combe)', OE.

Ilsham (Torquay): Possibly 'Hedgehog village', OE. (Hedgehog may have been a nickname!)

Ilsington: 'Ielfstan or Aefsige's farm', OE personal name plus *tun.*

Indescombe (Tavistock): 'Giant's Valley', OE.

Instow: 'Saint John's holy place', OE. Recorded *Jonestow* (1242) from church dedication. (See Jacobstowe, Petrockstow, etc.)

Inwardleigh: 'Inwar's woodland clearing'. Inwar (Norse name) held the manor in DB.

Ipplepen: 'Ipela's fold' OE personal name + OE *penn* (not to be confused with British penn meaning 'hill, head, end, chief').

Ivybridge: One of relatively few names that make perfect sense in modern English. Recorded *Ivebrugge* 1292 from OE *Ifg* + *brycg.*

J

Jacobstowe: 'Holy place of St Jacob (James)'. Church dedication to St James + *stow.* (See Churchstow, Instow and Christow.)

Jurston (in Chagford parish): 'Jordan's farm (*tun*)'.

K

Kelly: 'Grove, small wood'. Probably Cornish *kelli*.

Kenn (river): Uncertain. Pre-English, may be British 'brilliant, white'.

Kentisbeare: 'Centel's grove', OE personal name + *bearu*.

Kenton: 'Farm or settlement on river Kenn' (above).

Kerswell: 'Cress Stream' (see Kingskerswell). There are 6 Kerswells in Devon.

Killerton: Possibly 'Farm of Cwyldhere's people', OE personal name with *ing* + *tun*.

Kilmington: 'Cynehelm's farm or settlement', OE.

Kings Tamerton (Plymouth): 'King's farm/settlement on the river Tamar', OE. (See Tamar and Tamerton Foliot.)

Kingsbridge: 'The King's Bridge', OE. Remarkably little changed: recorded as *Cinges bricge* in 962, when the bridge linked two estates belonging to the king.

Kingskerswell: 'Spring or stream where watercress grows'. OE *caerse* + *wella*. The manor belonged to the king in DB. (See Abbotskerswell and Kerswell.)

Kingsteignton: 'King's farm (*tun*) on the river Teign'. Possessed by the king in DB. (See Teign.)

Kingston: 'King's farm or settlement', OE.

Kingswear: 'The king's weir', OE *cyning* + *wer*. (See Countess Wear.)

Knackers Knowle (near Washbourne): 'Knacker's hillock' (OE *cnoll*). 'Knacker' once meant confidence tickster. (See Crownhill.)

Knightshayes: Probably 'Enclosure of the young noblemen/retainers', OE *cnihts* + *haeg*. (See Chudleigh Knighton.)

Knowstone: 'Cnut's stone', OE personal name + OE *stan*.

L

Lambhay Street (Plymouth): 'Lamb enclosure', OE *haeg*.

Landkey: 'St Ke's church site', Cornish *lan*.

Larkbeare: 'Lark's grove', OE. Name of village and an Exeter street.

Laughter Hole and **Laughter Tor (Dartmoor):** Possibly British, corresponding to Welsh *llethr* and Cornish *ledr* 'slope, cliff, declivity'. This may also explain Leather Tor.

Lee and Leigh: Two spellings of same word, OE *leah,* 'woodland clearing'. (28 such places are listed in PND and many more in combination; see Lustleigh, Goodleigh, Chawleigh, etc.)

Leigham (Plymouth): 'Village at the woodland clearing' or 'Village at the fallow land', OE.

Lemon (river): Probably 'Elm river', British. (See Lowman.)

Lew (river): Possibly 'Bright stream', British.

Lewtrenchard: The Trenchard family were here in the 13th century.

Lifton: 'Farm or settlement on river Lew' (above).

Lillicrap (Sourton): Probably associated with Peter Lillicrop (meaning 'Whitehead'), recorded in parish 1330.

Littlehempston: 'Haeme's farm', OE personal name + *tun.* *Lytel* to distinguish it from Broadhempston (see above).

Littleham: 'Little hemmed in land', OE *lytel* + *hamm.*

Livermead (Torquay): 'Wild iris meadow', OE *maed*, Modern English mead. (See Meadfoot.)

Livery Dole (Exeter): 'Leofhere's share of the common field', OE.

Loddiswell: 'Lod's spring or stream', OE personal name + *wella.*

Longbrook Street (Exeter): From the stream that flowed at its foot. Originally a Roman road from East Gate to Pennsylvania (below).

Lowman (river): Probably 'Elm river', British. (See Lemon.)

Lundy: 'Puffin Island', ON. The puffins are still there.

Luppitt: 'Luffa's pit', OE.

Lustleigh: 'Leofgiest's clearing', OE personal name plus *leah.*

Lustleigh Cleave: 'Cliff or steep slope', OE *cleve.* A classic topographical name. (See Heddon's Mouth Cleave.)

Lyd (river): OE 'Noisy stream'.

Lydford: 'Ford on the Lyd', OE.

Lyme (river): 'Stream', British.

Lympstone: 'Leofwine's farm', OE personal name plus *tun.*

Lyn (river): OE 'Torrent'. The Lyn flooded swiftly and violently in 1952, killing 34 people.

Lynmouth: 'Mouth of the Lyn', OE.

Lynton: 'Farm on the Lyn', OE.

M

Magdalen Street (Exeter): From the ancient leper hospital of St Mary Magdalen. Recorded *Maudeleynestrete* 1419, it was pronounced 'Maudlin' (as in Magdalen College, Oxford).

Maidencombe: 'Maidens' valley', OE *combe*.

Mamhead: 'Breast-shaped hill', *mam* British, *heafod* OE.

Manaton: Either 'Manna's farm/settlement' (OE personal name + *tun*) or 'farm/settlement held communally' (OE *gemana*, 'common').

Marldon: 'Hill where gentian grows', OE.

Marsh Mills (Plymouth): The marsh covered most of the valley on the Egg Buckland side of the river Plym and along the tributary that fed Efford Mill. (See Efford, Egg Buckland and Plym.)

Martinhoe: 'Rocky spur belonging to Matta's people', OE. (See Hoe, Trentishoe and Mortehoe.)

Mary Tavy: See Tavy.

Meadfoot (Torquay): 'Meadow's foot'. (See Livermead.)

Meavy: Takes its name from the River Meavy, probably a British river name 'lively stream'.

Meeth: 'Junction of the rivers of streams', OE.

Membury: 'Fortified place' OE – the first element is uncertain.

Merrivale: 'Pleasant open place', OE.

Michelcombe: 'Big valley', OE.

Milk Street (Exeter): Street where milk was sold.

Millbay (Plymouth): Originally *Sourpolemylle* ('Sour Pool Mill') because of the brackish water which powered the tidal mill.

Milton: 'Middle farm or settlement', OE.

Milton Damerel: Held by Robert de Albemarle in DB.

Milton Abbot: Held by Tavistock Abbey. Latin *abbas* = abbot.

Modbury: 'Fortified meeting place' from OE *bury* + *gemot*, related to moot 'meeting or assembly'. (See Mutley.)

Molton, North and South: 'Farm or settlement' with (possibly) an unidentified hill name. The Moltons may have given the river Mole its name.

Monkleigh: 'Monks' woodland clearing', monk + *leah*. The village was held by Montacute Priory in the 12th century.

Monkleigh: In Monkokehampton parish is 'the monks' cliff' – monk + *cleve*, cliff or steep slope, as proved by early spelling *Monkeclyve* (1333). (See Lustleigh Cleave.)

Monkokehampton: 'Monks' estate on the river Okement'. It belonged to Glastonbury Abbey. (See Okement.)

Morchard Bishop: 'Great Wood' British *mor* + *ced*, owned by Bishops of Exeter. It was probably part of the same great wood as Cruwys Morchard (above).

Moreleigh: 'Moor wood or clearing', OE.

Moretonhampstead: 'Moor farm settlement', OE, one of 45 Moretons and Mortons recorded in England. Why the later 'homestead' was added is not known.

Mortehoe: 'Hill spur (OE *hoh*) called Mort or the stump', hence Morte Point. (See Hoe, Trentishoe, Martinhoe.)

Morice Town (Plymouth): From Sir William Morice, who bought the manor of Stoke in 1667 from Sir Charles Wise. (See Mount Wise below.)

Mothecombe: 'Valley at the mouth'. The valley (combe) opens into the Erme estuary at its mouth (*mutha*).

Mount Batten (Plymouth): From the Civil War governor of the fort here, Admiral Sir William Batten. Earlier, it was called Hostert, 'end of the promontory'. Lord Louis Mountbatten's father, Prince Louis of Battenberg, adopted the 'Mountbatten' family name to avoid anti-German sentiment in 1917.

Mount Gould (Plymouth): From Colonel William Gould, Governor of Plymouth's Civil War garrison.

Mount Radford (Exeter): Probably from association with Nicholas Radford, a 15th century Recorder of Exeter.

Mount Wise (Plymouth): Named after the Wise or Wyse family, owners of Stoke manor.

Mouse Hole or Mousehole: In Payhembury parish, first recorded 1586. Probably a contemptuous nickname, referring to a small place, whereas Mousehole, Cornwall, originally referred to a cave.

Musbury: 'Old fortification infested with mice', OE.

Mutley (Plymouth): Possibly 'meeting place at the clearing', OE *gemot + leah*. (See Modbury.)

N

Ness (Shaldon): 'Promontory or headland', ON *nes*. (See Totnes.)

Newton: 'New farm or settlement', OE. A very common place and surname.

Newton Abbot: 'The abbot's new farm or settlement'. Owned by Torre Abbey, 12th century.

Newton Bushel: Held by the Bussel family, 1329. (Newton Bushel and Newton Abbot were not fully amalgamated until 1901.)

Newton Ferrers: In 1306 William de Ferrers held the manor. 'Ferrers' is Norman, 'the smith or farrier'. (See Churston Ferrers and Bere Ferrers.)

Newton Poppleford: 'Pebble ford' – it is on the banks of the river Otter. The 'Newton' part of the name is not recorded before 1305.

Newton St Cyres: From church dedication.

Newton St Petrock: Granted to St Petrock's monastery, Bodmin, in 938 by King Athelestan.

Newton Tracy: Was held by Henry de Tracy, 1242. (See Nymet Tracy and Bovey Tracey.)

Northcott: 'Northern cottages', OE *cot*. There are 6 in Devon. (See Endicott, Westacott, Eastacott, Uppacott.)

Northam: 'North homestead or village (*ham*)', OE.

Northernhay (Exeter): Complements Southernhay (below) as the northern enclosure (OE *haeg*) of Exeter. (See Bonhay and Shilhay.)

Northleigh: 'Northern woodland clearing', OE. (See Southleigh.)

Northlew: From the river Lew (above), possibly 'bright stream', British.

Noss Mayo: 'Matthew's promontory', recorded as *Nesse Matheu*, 1286, when Matheu held the manor. Mayo is the Old French form of Matthew. Noss (ON – see Ness above) stands on a point of land between two creeks.

Notte Street (Plymouth): Originally Nut Street, presumably referring to nut trees.

Nymet Tracy: 'Sacred grove', British. Nimet may also be an old name for the river Yeo. Owned by de Tracy family, 13th century. (See Nympton, Bovey Tracey and Newton Tracy.)

Nymet Rowland: Owned by Roland, 12th century (see above).

Nympton: 'Farm or settlement on the river Nymet'. Derived from British *nimet* (see Nymet Tracey above), *Nymet* may also be an old name for the river Mole. At George Nympton the church is dedicated to St George. King's Nympton was a royal manor. Bishop's Nympton was held by the Bishops of Exeter.

O

Oddicombe (Torquay): 'Odda's valley', OE personal name + *cumb*.

Ogwell (East and West): 'Wocga's spring or stream', OE personal name + *wella*.

Okehampton: 'Farmstead on the river Okement'.

Okement: British river name – possibly 'swift stream'. (See Monkokehampton.)

Oldstone (Blackawton): 'Ulf's Farm', ON personal name + *tun*.

Otter (river): 'Otter', OE *oter*. The fish-eating mammals have recently re-colonised the river.

Otterton: 'Farmstead (*tun*) on the river Otter'.

Ottery St Mary: 'Otter stream', OE *oter* + *ea* (water) + church dedication.

P

Paignton: 'Farm or settlement connected with Paega', OE personal name + *ing* + *tun*.

Pancrasweek: 'St Pancras's specialised farm', OE. (See Week.)

Paris Street (Exeter): Formerly Shitbrook ('dirty brook') Street from the stream (now buried and used as a storm sewer) that flowed at the bottom. Origin uncertain.

Parliament Street (Exeter): The narrowest street in Exeter, nicknamed 'Squeezebelly'. Although medieval, its name dates from 1832 and the Reform Bill.

Parracombe: Possibly 'The peddler's valley (combe)' or 'enclosure valley', OE.

Payhembury: 'Paie's (OE personal name) high fortification'. (See Broadhembury.)

Pennsylvania (Exeter): Commemorates the US colony (later state) established by a Quaker, William Penn. Pennsylvania Terrace (now Pennsylvania Park) was financed by Mr Sparkes, a Quaker, in 1822. Later, the whole district was called Pennsylvania.

Pennycomequick (Plymouth): Disputed. It may have been copied from Falmouth, where an inn of that name was established about 1600. The origin at Falmouth seems to have been *Pen-y-cwm-cuik*, Cornish, head of a wooded valley, but the evidence is unreliable.

Peter Tavy: See Tavy.

Petrockstow: 'Holy place of St Petroc'. Cornish saint's name + OE *stow*. (See Christow, Churchstow, Instow, Jacobstowe.)

Peverell (Plymouth): A modern name derived from Weston Peverel (below).

Pinhoe: Possibly 'pin-shaped hill spur (*hoh*)' or 'hill spur called pen' from British *penn* = hill. (See Hoe.)

Pizwell: Recorded 1305 as Pishull, 'hill where peas are grown'.

Plym (river): Named after Plympton (below), which lies on its eastern bank.

Plymouth: 'Mouth (mutha) of the Plym', OE. Plymouth takes its name from the Plym, which in turn took its name from Plympton. (See Plympton and Sutton.)

Plymouth Sound: 'Sound' in the sense of 'channel' has been used since the 13th century. In OE it meant 'place for swimming'.

Plympton: 'Plum tree farm', OE *plyme* + *tun*. See Plym above.

Plymstock: Either 'Outlying plum tree farm' or 'Plympton's outlying farm', OE *plyme + stock*.

Plymtree: 'Plum tree', OE *plyme + treow*. This East Devon village is far from the river Plym.

Polsloe (Exeter): 'Poll's Marsh', derived from Polsloe Priory, built on low lying land owned by a Saxon called Poll.

Portlemouth (East): Possibly 'Harbour estuary' or 'Mouth of the harbour stream'.

Postbridge: The famous clapper bridge is medieval. 'Post' was probably added when it began to carry the post road. Recorded as 'Post Bridge' in 1675.

Poughill: 'Pohha's hill' or 'Bag-shaped hill', OE.

Powderham: 'Promontory on hemmed in marshy land', OE.

Prawle Point, East and West Prawle: 'Look-out hill', OE.

Preston: 'Priests' farm', OE. There are 10 Prestons in Devon.

Princetown: Modern settlement, established by Thomas Tyrwhitt, who named it in honour of the Prince of Wales, later George IV (1820-30), who owned much of Dartmoor as Duke of Cornwall.

Putford (East and West): Either 'Putta's ford' or 'Hawk ford', OE.

Pyworthy: 'Enclosure infested with gnats', OE. (See Beaford for another insect name.)

R

Rackenford: Possibly 'Ford suitable for riding,' or 'Ford of the gullies', OE.

Rat Combe (in Sampford Courtenay parish): Probably 'Red Valley.'

Rattery: 'The place at the red tree', OE *read* ('red' – giving the common surname Reed) and *treow* ('tree'). It has nothing to do with rats.

Revelstoke: 'Outlying farm or settlement', OE *stoc* + family name. The Revels were an important county family from 12th century.

Ringmore: Either 'Reedy moor' or, possibly, 'cleared moor', OE. There are two Ringmores in Devon. Ringmoor (in Sheepstor parish) has the same derivation.

Roborough: 'Rough hill or mound', OE.

Rockbeare: 'Rook grove', OE *hroc* + *bearu*.

Romansleigh: 'Woodland clearing', OE *leah* + church dedication to British Saint Rumon. There is no Roman connection.

Rougemont (Exeter): 'Red hill' in French, from the colour of the underlying rock. Exeter Castle was started in 1068, but not recorded as Rougemont until 1250.

Rousdon: 'Ralph's hill' was held by the Ralph family in 12th century + OE *dun*.

S

Saddle Tor: Named, like several Dartmoor tors, from its shape.

St Budeaux: 'St Budoc's hide', a British church dedication. OE *hid* (land measurement – see Combeinteignhead), given in medieval spellings, was lost from 1520.

St Sidwells (Exeter): The virgin Saint Sidfulle ('virtuous one') is said to have been buried near Exeter.

St Mary Church (Torquay): Ancient church dedication, 1050.

Salcombe: 'Salt valley', OE *sealt* + *cumb*. Salcombe Regis was a royal possession – Latin *regis* = of the king. (See Budleigh Salterton.)

Saltram: Probably 'Salters' settlement or hemmed in land', OE.

Sampford Courtenay: 'Sandy ford' (over the river Taw). Associated with the Courtenays since 1242. OE *sand* + *ford*.

Sampford Peverell: 'Sandy ford', held by the Peverel family in 12th century. (See Weston Peverel.)

Sampford Spiney: 'Sandy ford', held by the Spiney family in 13th century.

Sandford: As Sampford. Recorded *Sandforda* in 930, it shows remarkable continuity.

Satterleigh: 'Robbers' woodland clearing', OE.

Saunton: 'Farm by the sands', OE.

Seaton: 'Sea farm or settlement', OE.

Shaldon: The first element 'Shal' is obscure, but the second is OE *dun*, 'hill'. (See Ness.)

Shaugh Prior: 'Small wood', OE. It belonged to Plympton Priory.

Shebbear: 'Grove where the shafts or poles are got', OE.

Sheepstor: 'Craggy hill (torr) resembling a bar, bolt or dung', OE.

Sheepwash: 'A place to wash sheep.' There are three Devon places, all near rivers, one by the Torridge (Sheepwash), one by the Nymet (in Bishop's Nympton parish), one by the river Wash (Washbourne, Halwell parish).

Shillingford: Probably 'Sciella's people at the ford', OE, or 'Ford over the noisy stream', OE.

Shiphay: 'Sheep enclosure', OE. There are three places of this name in Devon.

Shitbrook (Exeter): 'Dirty stream', OE. (See Paris Street.)

Shobrooke: 'Brook haunted by an evil spirit', OE.

Shute: Uncertain, possibly 'Corner of land' or 'Steep slope'. There are six instances in Devon.

Silverton: Probably 'gully ford farm or settlement', OE.

Sid (river): 'Wide', OE. Wide has always been a relative term. The modest Sid is wider than some rivers.

Sidbury: 'Fortified place on the river Sid', OE. Sidbury village is overlooked by a large Iron Age hillfort.

Sidford: 'Ford on the Sid', OE.

Sidmouth: 'At the mouth of the Sid', OE.

Silverton: Probably 'Gully ford farm or settlement', OE.

Slapton: 'Slippery (or possibly muddy) farm or settlement', OE.

Slapton Ley: 'Slapton's lake or pool', OE.

Smythen Street (Exeter): Street where smiths worked, first recorded circa 1150. The top end was called Butcher's Row until the late 19th century – again a trade name.

Snapper: 'Boggy land', OE *snaep* as in Snape Marshes, Suffolk.

Sourton: 'Farm or settlement on a neck of land', OE.

South Brent: 'Southern high or steep place', British. (See Brentor.)

South Hams: Hamm signifies land hemmed in by water, marsh or higher ground; Hams means villages. Both OE words *Ham* and

Hamm are altogether apt for the villages of South Devon, known collectively as 'the South Hams'.

South Zeal: OE sele, 'The willow tree'. (See Zeal Monachorum.)

Southcott: 'Southern cottages', OE. There are 11 in Devon. (See Northcott, Westacott, Uppacott, Eastacott.)

Southernhay (Exeter): Complements Northernhay (above) as the southern enclosure (OE *haeg*) of Exeter. (See Bonhay and Shilhay.)

Southleigh: 'Southern woodland clearing'. It is recorded as *Lega* in DB and *Suthlege* in 1242, distinct from nearby Northleigh. Southleigh parish is still well wooded, Northleigh less so.

Southside Street (Plymouth): Led to Southside Quay in Sutton Harbour (below).

Sowton: 'South farm or settlement', OE. Comparable with Sutton (below). Sowton was recorded as *Clis* in DB, after the river Clyst.

Sparkwell: 'Stream or spring where brushwood grows', OE.

Starcross: Said to be derived from a cross erected by the monks of Sherborne Abbey at the foot of the ferry steps. Absence of early spellings makes it impossible to be certain.

Start: 'Tongue of land, promontory', OE. Mabel de Sturte lived at Start, 1333.

Staverton: 'Farm or settlement' beside 'ford marked by posts', OE.

Stepcote Hill (Exeter): Probably 'The Steep Street', OE, not the stepped street – though the steps remain. This was the original main street into the medieval city from West Gate.

Sticklepath: 'Steep hill', OE. Sticklepath Hill, Barnstaple, has the same meaning as the Dartmoor village.

Stockleigh English: Probably 'Tree stump clearing', OE *stocc* + *leah* (not to be confused with Stoke, see below). It was held by the Engles family.

Stockleigh Pomeroy: 'Tree stump clearing' held by the Pomerei family. (See Berry Pomeroy.)

Stoke: 'An outlying farm or settlement'. OE *stoc*. Found, with minor variations, in 35 Devon place names.

Stoke Canon: Held by canons of Exeter monastery.

Stoke Damerel (Plymouth): The manor was held by Robert de Albarmarla, 1086.

Stoke Gabriel: Church dedication to Saint Gabriel.

Stoke Fleming: Manorial family name le Flemeng ('of Flanders'). The same family held Bratton Fleming (above).

Stokeinteignhead: 'Outlying farmstead in the district containing ten hides', OE. Despite the spelling, there is no connection in the place name to the nearby river Teign. (See Combeinteignhead.)

Stokenham: 'Outlying farm or settlement in the South Hams' (see above). Recorded as Stoke in Hamm in 1276. OE *stoc + hamm*.

Stonehouse (Plymouth): The OE name is self-explanatory, but why should the Saxons, who built chiefly in wood, have used it? Perhaps they uncharacteristically built a stone house themselves or found a stone house (or its ruins) built by Romans or Romanised Britons here?

Stoodleigh: 'Woodland clearing for keeping a horse herd', OE.

Stowford: 'Stony ford', OE.

Strete: 'Place on the old (usually Roman) road', OE. Strete near Slapton is on a main road, possibly an ancient trackway, but Street in Branscombe parish is not and was the home of William atte Strete, 1333.

Strete Raleigh (Whimple parish): It lies near an old Roman road (see Strete) from Exeter to Dorchester – but it may be named from a more ancient trackway. Henry de Ralegh held the manor in 1242.

Sutton: 'South farm (*tun*)'. The original name of Plymouth, now only applied to Sutton Harbour and Sutton Pool. In medieval times there were two manors of Sutton – Sutton Prior, held by Plympton Priory, and Sutton Vautort, held by the Vautort (Valletort) family – see Valletort Road. There are four other Suttons in Devon. (Sutton is a common surname. See also Sowton.)

Swincombe: 'Swine valley (*combe*)', OE. There are three in Devon.

T

Talaton: 'Farm or settlement on river Tale', OE (see below).

Tale (river): 'Quick, active, swift', OE.

Tamar (river): Possibly 'The dark one' or simply 'River', British. (See Tavy.)

Tamerton Foliot: 'Farm/settlement on the river Tamar'. The Foliot family were here in 13th century. (See King's Tamerton.)

Tavistock: 'Outlying farm or settlement (OE *stoc*) on the Tavy'. (See Tavy.)

Tavy (river): Similar British root to Tamar (above). Possibly 'Dark one' or simply 'River'. Mary Tavy and Peter Tavy, both near the Tavy, derive from their church dedications.

Taw (river): Possibly 'Strong or silent stream', British. (See Bishop's Tawton and Tawstock.)

Tawstock: 'Outlying farm/settlement (OE *stoc*) on the Taw' (see above).

Tawton (North and South): 'Farm/settlement on the Taw' (OE *tun*).

Tedburn St Mary: 'Tatta's stream', OE personal name (possibly female) + *burna* 'stream' + church dedication.

Teign (river): 'Stream', British.

Teigngrace: From the Teign (above). Held by the Gras family in the 14th century.

Teignmouth: 'Mouth of the Teign' (above).

Thelbridge: 'Plank bridge', OE.

Thorverton: 'Farmstead by a ford, marked by a thorn tree' or 'Thurferth's farmstead', OE.

Throwleigh: 'Woodland clearing by a conduit', OE.

Thurlestone: 'Holed rock', OE, referring to the notable rock just offshore.

Thrushel (river): Derived from Thrushelton (below).

Thrushelton: 'Farm/settlement frequented by thrushes', OE.

Titchberry: 'Tetti's fortification', OE personal name + *burh*. (See Tedburn.)

Tiverton: 'Double ford farm or settlement', OE, *Twyfyrde* 880. Tiverton is at the confluence of the rivers Exe and Lowman.

Topsham: Probably 'Topp's hemmed in land', OE. Topsham, almost at the confluence of the Exe and Clyst, is surrounded by water and marsh, making it a good example of a name with *hamm*.

Tor: 'Rocky hill', OE *torr* (see separate entries for Hound Tor, Saddle Tor and other Dartmoor tors).

Torbryan: 'Rocky hill' + Norman family manorial name de Brione.

Torcross: Associated with two families, Walter de la Torre (1281) and Adam de la Cros (1316). The Tor might be the promontory south of the village. However, the nearest cross is one mile inland at Mattiscombe.

Torquay: 'Quay by the rocky hill' (OE *torr* below). Recorded as *Torrekay* 1591, it grew in the ancient parish of Tormoham, held by the de Mohun family, 1242.

Torre (Torquay): Similar to tor, 'The rocky hill', OE, it gives Torwood (*Torrewood* 1574) and later Torwood Street and Torwood Gardens.

Torridge (river): 'Rough stream', British.

Torrington Black, Great and **Little:** 'Farm or settlement (OE *tun*) on the Torridge' (see above). 'Black' refers to the river.

Totnes: 'Totta's promontory', OE personal name + *naess* – referring to the mound (a volcanic plug) on which the castle stands. (See Ness.)

Trentishoe: 'Round hill spur', OE. (See Hoe.)

Trumpeter (Ilsington parish): From *Tromptsmede* – 'The mead (meadow) of one called Trump'.

Tuckenhay: 'Oak enclosure', recorded *Tokenhey* 1550. OE, possibly combination of *aet* ('at'), *oke* ('oak') and *haeg* ('enclosure').

Turnchapel (Plymouth): 'St Anne's Chapel' was recorded as 'Tan Chapel' in 1765, and further corrupted to Turnchapel.

Twitchen: 'At the cross roads', OE. Seven places in Devon.

U

Uffculme: 'Uffa's estate on the river Culm', OE personal name + British river name. (See Culm.)

Ugborough: 'Ugga's hill or mound', OE personal name + *beorg*.

Upcott: 'Higher cottages', OE *cot*. There are 39 Upcotts in Devon, plus 3 Uppacotts, making it one of the county's most common names.

Uplowman: 'Higher up the river Lowman'. (See Lowman.)

Uplyme: 'Higher up the river Lyme'. (See Lyme.)

Upottery: 'Higher up the river Otter'. (See Otter.)

Upton: 'Higher farmstead or village', OE.

Upton Hellions: Held by William de Helihun (a Breton name), 1242.

Upton Pyne: Held by the de Pyn family, 13th century.

V

Valletort Road (Plymouth): The Valletort family had a long association with Plymouth, beginning with Renaldus de Valletort, given the manor of Plymouth by Henry I, 1135.

Vauxhall Street (Plymouth): A corruption of 'Foxhole'.

Venn: 'Marshy land', OE *fenn*. There are 30 such names in Devon, where 'f' is usually pronounced 'v'.

Venn Ottery: 'Marshy land by the river Otter'. (See Otter.)

Venlake: 'Fen lake', OE.

Virginstow: 'St Bridget the Virgin's holy place'. Church dedication + OE *stow*. (See Instow, Churchstow, and Christow.)

W

Walkham (river): 'Rolling one', OE.

Walkhampton: Probably 'Farmstead of the people who dwell by the Walkham', OE.

Walreddon (Whitchurch parish): 'Community of Britons', OE *walh* 'Briton'. Significantly, Walreddon is near the Cornish border.

Warfleet (Dartmouth): Probably OE 'Rampart by the creek' and not derived from warships anchored at Dartmouth.

Washbourne: 'Sheep-wash stream', OE. (See Sheepwash.)

Watcombe: 'Wheat valley', OE.

Waterbeer Street (Exeter): From water bearers or carriers.

Weare Gifford: 'Weir' held by the Giffard family in 13th century. (See Compton Gifford and Aveton Gifford.)

Week(e): 'Dwelling', 'hamlet' or 'village' in its general sense, but usually 'specialised farm or trading settlement', OE *wic*. There are 23 Weeks in Devon.

Well: 'Spring or stream', OE *wella*.

Welcombe: 'Spring/stream valley', OE *wella* + *cumb*. (See Woolacombe.)

Wembury: Uncertain. 'Holy', 'tumour shape' and 'wagon' have been offered for first element. All authorities agree second element is OE *burh*, 'fortification'.

Wembworthy: 'Wemba's enclosure', OE personal name + *worthig*.

Westacott: 'West cottages', OE *cot*. There are 26 instances in Devon. (See related Endicott, Northcott, and Upcott etc.)

Weston Peverel (Plymouth): 'West farm or settlement'. The Peverel family were connected with the place from 1228. (See Sampford Peverell and Peverell.)

Westward Ho! Victorian seaside village with two distinctions. It is the only English settlement called after a novel – Charles Kingsley's *Westward Ho!* (1855) was largely set in the area – and is the only settlement name in England with an exclamation mark.

Whimple: 'White pool or stream'. Village name from a British stream name.

Whipton: 'Wippa's farm or settlement', OE personal name + *tun*.

Whitchurch: 'White church', OE, possibly indicating 'stone church', to distinguish it from the majority of Saxon churches, which were in wood or cob.

Whitleigh (Plymouth): 'White woodland clearing', OE.

Widecombe in the Moor: 'Willow valley' or 'wide valley', OE. The minor names Widdacombe and Widdicombe have the same possible meanings.

Wilmington: 'Wilhelm's farm or settlement', OE.

Winkleigh: Either 'Wineca's clearing' or 'corner clearing', OE.

Witheridge: Either 'Willow ridge' or 'wether-sheep ridge', OE.

Wolsdon Street (Plymouth): Where the wool dressers lived. Medieval artisans usually grouped together.

Wonford: Probably British, *gwyn ffrwd* 'white stream'.

Woodbury: 'Fort by the wood', OE *wudu* + *burh*.

Woodbury Salterton: 'Salt workers farm', OE *saltere* + *tun*. (See Budleigh Salterton.)

Woolacombe: 'Valley with a spring or stream', OE *wiella* + *cumb*. (See Welcombe.)

Woolfardisworthy: (Pronounced Woolsery) 'Wulfheard's enclosure', OE personal name + *worthig*. There are two in Devon.

Worlington (East and West): 'Wulfraed's farm/settlement', OE personal name + *ing* + *tun*.

Wreyland: From the Wray Brook, possibly 'felon stream', OE.

Y

Yarnscombe: 'Eagle's valley', OE.

Yarcombe: 'Yarty valley'.

Yarty (river): Like several ancient river names, its meaning defies explanation.

Yealmpton: 'Farm/settlement (OE *tun*) on the Yealm' (pronounced 'Yam'). British river name, uncertain meaning.

Yelverton: Recorded as *Elleford* in 1291, 'Elder tree ford', OE. *Tun* was added later.

Yeo (name of several rivers): 'Water', OE. However, the Yeo that joins the Creedy (above) may be 'Yew stream'.

Z

Zeal Monachorum: 'Place at the willow belonging to the monks', OE *sele* + *monachorum* (Latin, 'of the monks') referring to its possession by Buckfast Abbey. (See South Zeal and Buckland Monachorum.)

A Brief Bibliography

Cameron, Kenneth, *English Place Names*, Batsford, 1996. Gives a balanced overall picture of the subject.

English Place Name Society's annual Journal, Nottingham. Provides academic articles keeping readers up to date with new developments.

Ekwall, Eilert, *The Concise Oxford Dictionary of English Place Names*, Oxford, 1960. Still an excellent reference, but largely overtaken by Mills and Watts (below).

Gelling, Margaret and Cole, Ann, *The Landscape of Place Names*, Shaun Tyas, Stamford, 2000. Investigates a crucial area of place name studies and provides many examples.

Gover, JEB, Mawer, A and Stenton, FM, *The Place Names of Devon*, English Place Name Society, Nottingham, 1931 and 1998 (two volumes). Inevitably dated, but by far the most comprehensive book on Devon place names.

Mills, AD, *Oxford Dictionary of English Place Names*, Oxford, 1998. Excellent and reasonably priced, with a useful introduction.

Mills, AD, *Oxford Dictionary of British Place Names*, Oxford, 2003. Extended and updated version of the above.

Watts, Victor, *Cambridge Dictionary of English Place Names*, Cambridge, 2004. The most thorough study to date. Priced as a reference library book.

Websites

University of Nottingham Institute for Name Studies is one of the best and most authoritative sites.
The section on Devon names is especially helpful:
www.nottingham.ac.uk/english/ins/about.htm

Genuki offers an essay on Devon place names:
http://genuki.cs.ncl.ac.uk/DEV/DevonMisc/Nomenclature.html

An essay on the history of English place names:
www.sca.org/heraldry/laurel/names/engplnam.html

Further enquiries: English Place Name Society, School of English Studies, University of Nottingham, Nottingham NG7 2RD. 0115 9515919. New members welcome. Source for other county place name volumes.
www.nottingham.ac.uk/english/ins/epns/